Comfortably on Purpose

Comfortably on Purpose

Mike Mandzik

ISBN: 979-8-9960540-0-8
Published by Westbrae Literary Group
Berkeley, California
Jon-David Hague, Founding Editor

For more information about this and other titles from
Westbrae Literary Group, visit us
at westbraeliterarygroup.com or email us at info@westbraeliterarygroup.com

Contents

From a Lockward Prompt

for my Diane

I was satisfied with a moment's glance
    until your smile eye-blued me
    to the bottom stair,
    a standing deer, frozen
    in your lash-lights,
    just a still shot,
    mugged one-off.

But now I want a marathon spectacular,
    an epic festival, a parade
    of pageantry, the voyage of a
    lifetime listing carelessly as
    the Maid of the Mist slips
    majestically, over the Falls.

No beginning, middle, end,
    bottom or top sails into view
    unless we tack the times
    with chances that each episode
    sounds another echo, fleetly
    passing for romance.

Should the rays of sun
    and stars expire, and of
    moon-glow wane or dim,
    we'll proceed with caution
    and our souls adrift, made
    full with radiant care. Amen.

Frozen Funds

My father never spent a red cent on anything he could make
    himself.
We did everything from residing our house with cedar shakes
 to giving the old Ford a tune up whenever it ran rough or was
    hard to start.

Since he fed and clothed me for all my early years, obviously he
    already
had overpaid for my services before I even knew how to do
    anything.
So on weekends, I was at his beck and call.

Winter dropped the curtain early on Saturday afternoons
in the driveway between our house and old Miss Gore's next
    door.
My chief job was holding the flashlight so he could see the spark
    plug

or whatever he wanted to tighten down. There were no
    floodlights outside.
The alleyway kept any streetlight out in the public domain,
and after a while all he said was, "Hold that goddamn light still,
    will ya!"

My frozen fingers tried to keep the beam steady but even the
    flashlight
was a block of ice and my gloves were soaked from snowball
    fights,
building forts and igloos. My feet were frozen and I really had to
    pee.

Sometimes the wrench broke free. He might skin a gloveless
    knuckle,
bark a vowel of pain, then reseat the tool (held tighter now in his
    fist)
and work the nut down, however long it took.

Mom would call us in for supper five or six times before he'd
    say,
"Okay, now check for tools in there before you turn off your
    light,"
and he latched the hood shut as only a child of the Depression
    knew how to do.

He handed me the box-end wrench to put away and I felt his
    cold fingers,
amazed that even the blood in the gash on his knuckle was
    frozen stiff
in its place, too scared to be spent without proper authorization.

More Shirts Than Money

a palimpsest from Gottshall

Sometimes I say I'm going to meet my brother at the fights—
even though I have no brother—just because it's such
a macho thing to say. I've always thought so, ever since

I saw on TV that two brothers said they always met together
at the fights. The other day, for example, I jogged alone
on the steaming track down at the high school, behind a pack

of regulars, thinking one of those shake-n-bakers might turn and
    ask me to catch up.
I had a water bottle and a wrist band. The homeroom bell broke
    on
silent muggy air. Summer shimmered horizontally over blacktop
    broiling

nothing. I brought a sleeve with heavy metal CD's down to the
    ring
and took a free towel from the uniformed usher. I like a place
where you can hear the sounds of strength at work

like the difference between lime and candle light,
and the price of fandom. It's going up. I watched
someone who could be my brother walk in through the gate,
    wipe the sweat

from his brow. I thought, even now the vendors are selling
souvenirs from their carts, tee shirts twenty bucks, two for
    thirty-four.
All over the city, any one of these brothers could be mine.

On "Oh"

(a movie short)

Oh no! Not that word!
That sound of smoke
rung out of mouth
about nothing,
out loud.

Dot hollowed, form spoked
open into round,
as stone drops
on to pond, toneless
toll of object
poverished from
bottom to top.

Worded bother,
retort of lost report.
You're gone
on, alone.
Plop. Pout. Closed.

Long song echo,
Done. Forest logged.
Poem recorded. Tome decoded.
Sore for love, souls unwound.
Clocks stopped—or not.

Hope floats, blown forward
over shoals. Boats
on ozone fathom sounds,

lots of chop as motor steamed
cross ocean. Old worlds
found for others. Beyond,
not omens, nor someone's
ornery moping, no. Only now.
So wow, you say, "oh."

Knowing Where the Dreams Ends

Watching the beach disappear beneath your feet one night,
I thought of trying to hold you and have the
both of us stand our ground. If we stood our ground,
I thought as I watched your feet
disappear into the beach that night,
we could have built a pier on that spot
to sail our dream ships. But starting from
forever, we'd shore up our ankles, drive them
like pilings to withstand pulling tides and beating surf
inevitably testing all who try to stop and stand the sea...
As the tide pulled sand past us, it bleached those thoughts
into unspoken words along the shoreline.

Being on the beach at two A.M. may have had to do with my
simple speculation. It was a stand-off situation we faced,
alone against the dull black waves with some friends
and sleeping fishermen further on up the surf.

We could have but we didn't. My words got caught in
the under tow, ebbed with grains of sand right off the beach.
Vacation ended and we headed back, left the Shore again.
At home another night, I watched as fog crept down off the
      mountain,
the ghost of rain, mist, salt spray. I saw the dreams I held
 from you down the Shore, the dreams I built on sand,
      weakened, still moist...
I saw them disappear again beneath our feet.

In that while since then,
Indian Summer has been left along earth's orbit,

Autumn set its torch to the Northern forests,
Winter Solstice has been reached.
This half of the world sits quiet in cold storage,
quiet as cool blue rain.
We move along as seasons counterpoint
our simple dreams, yet still we dream quieter than snow.

The sleeping bear in my bloodstream
hibernates with one eye open.
He watches, waiting for the fish to start up river,
when he'll wake again and eat his fill,
licking his paws as he roams dry land.

Black Friday

Here is what I got wrong.

Even though
he never showed
up again,

I was
the happiest
I'd ever been.

After smoldering with
fear—no, with perpetual
panic that wrapped me
like skin on a skeleton,

I decided to
bronze the hammock
for future tryptophan-induced
comatosers, plump full

of cranberry relish, sweet potatoes
and mashed smooth whites. Egg
timer clicks on windowsill
until bell rings, bird ready.

Pies stacked atop the breakfront,
nut bread loaf cooling on the porch,
nestled in a checkered dish towel
on an otherwise empty Adirondack chair.

I bear him no grudge despite
his now absence. The store-bought
devils food that he brought

last year was well-intended enough.
But all he did after dinner was sleep
and hog up the hammock, he did.

Next day, azaleas dropped
their leaves like Walt Whitman
on his way to Willowbrook Mall.

We should have bronzed them all.

The Branch and Shadow

"Did you wash that thing like I asked
you to, or did you forget?" Her question
grows another ring beneath my burling bark.
So now what's next, I mutter to myself.
Last week, an 800-pound gorilla
passed consensus on my candidacy,
that my answers were vague,
with not enough examples to qualify
as data-driven outcomes, obviously
proving myself their undesired B-player.
Since now I know that move was never
meant to be, this will be no loss
because we can learn from it.
I am not fit for that position,
come I to my own conclusion.
I am not out on a limb.
Too many times have I tried
to stretch myself to fit the bill
for places I thought were
where I thought I wanted to be,
if only because I was not there.
I reached out then like I was
running to a shadow,
but found only empty space
devoid of light
that was never there
to begin with.
Her washed item chimes cleaner
than a bell rung gently
in icy mountain air.

To Marion of Lion's Teeth

1.
The Muse, um, lives where she breathes,
where she folds and kneads her forms
drawn in spirit, sown and shorn
of naught but best intentions.
She does not fill vine
with grape so that wine
might mull or craft purpose
solely from need.
Her wanton mysteries daze,
from deeper in her lair,
out from *unter den Linden.*
She sparks, he thinks:
what would come if I cut this branch
and graft it thus, to the trunk? if I poked
this seed up in her womb,
what would come? might it bloom?

2.
      Moving On

Our first direction that morning
was into Reverse.
Slowly,
chopped livers shivered,
iced into buckets by frozen shovels.
Missed you barely through
the bottom holes.
You kicksparked the clock
forward into warmer time zones
with cooler latitudes.

Wow that's great, you said,
now shift into Drive
and step on the gas.

3.
Every day is Mother's Day
but especially in late Spring,
the month after forsythias
scream at me to clean up my room,
the month after my Mom's birthday,
when azaleas have popped out of buds,
when dogwoods' white veils wed young green trees,
when brilliant maroon Japanese maples
leave us warm in nurturing photons.

4.
One long task remains before me.
My clever heart is cluttered,
cleaving to all I would
clean from my veins.
My roots drill blind
in the cavity of the past.

Thirty-one years have gone,
pewtered frames of windows, passed.
Burdens buried with hopes of heaven
and you, my dearest mother still,
I could not hold you here.

Your happy laughter,
your screeched delight when
fits of sneezing caught you
breathless, left you gasping,
just about cackling, smiling.

You'd say, "It's the histamines!"
as you giggled into your napkin.
"Red wine has histamines,
and it's histamines make me sneeze!"

Your breathless smile, always wide
and open, like your arms akimbo,
welcoming any and everyone to your table,
your giving of thanks, for life,
for joy, for all to share.
Your smile left, you, breathless.

5.
Some days I fear that there are
more dandelions than Mandziks.
Wadded spores age all too well.
Draggly thickneck rootage drills
unfoiled until feast waters feed
capillarily forky green leaves,
wider than their longest sides, resting
soaked in wattage purely spread,
direct, or ambient, shaded, or
even all fogged up. Tragically,
there are in the world, some days,
more dandelions than Mandziks.

Suit Department Karma

1.
As far back as I can remember, nothing ever fit me right.
My pant cuffs were rolled up inside
like the too-big waist band,
tacked to my size with a few stitches.
My shirt sleeves got tucked up,
sewed so the cuffs just covered my wrists.
It looked like I had stripes between the elbows
and cuffs. And of course, the cuffs were folded back
and buttoned. One of my aunts puffed me up when she told me,
"When well-to-do men wore their shirts like this, they were
    called French cuffs."
Then one day, I learned this wasn't so. It can still take a while
    for truth to find me.
Moving along slow and steady, this is how it usually gets to me.
After which, it drops on me like a bushmaster from a tree.

2.
We all wear the scarf of regret.
Ants flattened underfoot while bringing food to the colony.
The last cigarette crushed in a tray. Lives, stubbed out of place,
yet not out of mind. Ashy residue floats from a smoking barrel.
Hand-made muffler collars chilled remembrance.
This silent wrap may not be entirely appropriate for swimwear.
Even more unthinkable is to be caught without it,
an unmentionable accessory to naked truth.

3.

The Milky Way
is permanent press,
meant to be lived in.
So how's the fit?
It's all in the way
that you treat people.
If done wrong,
the look is crumpled.
When it's done right,
you look like you belong.
Of course, some wrinkles are free,
comfortably on purpose.

Backspace

I need a day, at least
one day per week to sort
my bags of mental change
from fields of crumpled bills,

But that day must fall
before the wrens of Saturn
wring blood from stones
or heave the wrongs of Spring
and all is lost in a stack of needles.

The pitchfork with its twisted tine
holds the sea infrequent,
tunes a sextant,
flattens atonality.

Start on the last page.
Read from now to then.
Interject the leavened pages,
risen, folded, knead connection.

If A, then B,
no truer thought be told.

Logos cubes our final view,
streams Creation under dome
until Whispers crack agenda,
and Fictation roots our soul.

That dimension is no longer,
did not linger for a second,
The allied past is passed; has left us.
We are stuck here, future-struck.

Highland Fling

Its front mostly shaded by hemlock,
the cabin we bought
sat south of the lake.

Not next to it, mind you,
but too good a walk to take a swim,
or a dip, as you were prone to want.

You'd only go to the beach by car.
I'd lug our towels, your chair,
an old sheet to lie on,
and a cooler iced with beer and soda.

The day before we sold the place,
the edge of winter went damp.
Mildew poured out the door.

I bundled our sheets, towels and suits;
stuffed them all into my truck.
Left the chair out on the lawn.

The long way home rolled slow
down the unpaved mountain road
as gravel dropped off my tires.

Time's Mirror

Ekphratic on a painting by Barbara Patterson

The atmosphere blends moisture to spin
new a world awakening.
Trim tree shadows reflect deep
under dark-bottomed clouds once liquid.

And now these rafts of bulbous light
float to damp the sunrise,
as roiling gassy magma
spews photons for eternity.

Our twirling planet
juggles civilizations smoother
than a circling yo-yo walks the dog,
flips eons faster than eyelids flicker,
but quicker than the end of day
draws near the night,
it turns our point of view.

And then the evening will fold
this well-lit scene under fading light
into space-black eventually.

If day was but a hole in night,
the setting glow would paint all
bright and wrap this beauty
on a well-framed canvas
to hold its sight forever.

Chance of Passing

It rains like a truck full of ducks.
Before the truck bed lost its gaskets,
before the first load of backfill was bucketed in
and dumped out, the bedliner scraped and swept clean,
a cubic yard of water was found by ducks splashing downward,
landing on webbed feet, wet and loud, flapping
flockfulls of wetness onto fairings and bumpers.
It rains like paint sprayed from too far away; globbing spots
fill blank spaces until surfaces shine with dripping new coats,
smell of wet, and wait to dry until after your touch.
It rains like dust storms grate on skin.
It rains like an eggbeater; it rains like motors.
It rains like shoveled crushed stone,
strong armed, lifted and flung artlessly
over broad shirtless shoulders.
It rains like whispers through a warm humid night.
It rains like pursed curtains blown off a muggy wood sill.
It rains like Niagara, rolling, roaring, over and down.
It rains like a job fair flooded with prospects.
It rains like promises spoken by drought.

Back to Normal

Bed-headed, it smelled well rested.
Plans for the weekend were bright,
agleam. We planned the final clean out.
That's what *she* said.

Further down, fresh smoked beast
melted in the maw, but stopped short
of all it cracked up to be; far short.
That *is* what she said.

So, where was this normal,
she wanted to say.
Words hung clear,
on point to their iced end.

Tangentially, it does help
if you know what you want.
Immensely in fact,
and of infinite extent.

Our words blurred
into sounds heard underwater,
spun like spokes in wheels,
as meaning levels lifted and dropped,

helped down and out
by those unremarkable forces,
gravity and entropy.

Oval Sex

The egg balanced on the narrow end of the cosmos.
The monument memorialized the gavel strike.
The age was Ovaltine.
The creed was danced unbelievably in clear water.
The job was rigged to ride long distance.
The date was hump day, 1969.
The year between was unauthorized.
The pharmacist's niece was surgically altered.
The vehicle was recreational.
The transmission was manually autonomic.
The summer was riotous.
The thigh tops rowed from an eccentric pivot.
The mountain between us was unauthorized.
The pulse of bed creak quaked to climax.
The oracle stood by the reshape of time.
The gauge of truth was talked to death.

Wax Waned

The plowman turns
soil for bread.

Mad Icarus is fallen
from the heights.

His face all flushed
from the rush of blood.

Witness the wetness
warm to the touch.

Through a snake
of white cloud,

like a child of snow,
mad Icarus fell

from the heights
on his head.

Turkey Buzzard Tower

After Li Po

There perched in days past, gnashing buzzards, which nested the
    Wild Turkey Tower.
Many ages since removed, the Tower base crumbles with broken
    bottles, voided tobacco boxes.
Just off the ridge, the creek trace fills with rain.

Mills' Estate sported gardens near where blueberry brambles
    under saplings spread.
Wall gates admit moss beds. Stumps and stones settle deeper in
    ownerless boundary.
Hill slopes fold the western face. Runoff feeds Newark
    Reservoir.

Look northward. Two scraggy carapaces drop skyward off a
    higher hill on Garret Mountain.
Look away to the opposite, Eagle Rock and South Mountain
    spread their treefull reservations.
These three woodlands plus the place whence we look face a
    trim treed expanse

out east to where begins the Blacklands—there, the never-ending
    wayside wastes,
urban vertebrae idle gray and grape-soured under the smog
    brown-hazed horizon.
Off southeasterly, Pulaski Skyway spans the furthest reaches of
    Newark Bay

when it appears on relatively clear days,
such as this, prior to-fall.
But now illumined, while Sun scatters in treetop tangles

up on the western Watchung ridge,
a spirit-world twilights—soon, before Heaven's Eye opens out
and star flight soars, lost in gloom to the distant city.

The Lost Word

She found herself
to be well off the mark,
when in fact
she only wanted to be well off.
What choices did she need to make?

She's a lilac tree,
a bush of sweet truth,
a scent of spring clarity.
She's the stoppage of wrong,
the parser of time.

She sits on stony sands
near her mountain lake,
and trills a siren's song.

She's a lilac tree,
a bush of sweet truth,
the scent of spring clarity.

Nearby, the river drops
down slow to wet's immortal bed.
To whisper, gnash, or garnish sleep,

she's a lilac tree,
the bush of sweet truth,
the scent of spring clarity.

Full throated, her voice assures.
With empurpled hair,
she takes her mark.

She is the stoppage of wrong,
the parser of time.
Her blue-brain drifts amazed.

The lilac tree,
the bush of sweet truth,
the scent of spring clarity.

Lunch with Jimmy Sturr

A few of my relatives from the old country
were illiterate yet multilingual immigrants.
Life back there was not so very good
that they wanted to keep speaking their native tongue.
Rather like cooler months that needed less shade,
they shed their language like falling leaves,
glad for gravity & the earth's rotation,
and polkas from the kitchen transistor radio on Sunday
        afternoons.

Annually, after our autumnal apple picking expeditions,
we always tried to find a family-friendly place to eat.
In the years before any of us had kids we weren't so picky,
but add a couple of cranky toddlers to the bunch
and we felt that our dining choices were less than in previous
        years.
The kids could barely walk back then, so we packed them up
and started off to create our own new tradition.
Luckily, we found the Jolly Onion in Pine Island.
Our table was right next to Jimmy Sturr and his band.
We knew we'd eat well here.

Every year, apple trees bared their limbs but, on that warm fall
        day,
not before we'd picked our bushels-full.
We wanted enough fruit to bake some pies,
some cobbler perhaps and have some left to eat.
The first years we went picking, we brought back so many bags
that even after baking, saucing, eating and sharing with
        everyone,

we still had some go soft. Then the kids grew older
and we started skipping trips. Now, the warm baked pies
are full of farm stand fruit.

And now, although I can think
universal thoughts with eclectic particulars,
I trudge like a circling pony,
shod and saddled, tricked into believing that,
because my opposable digits dip & dance across
well-designed hand-held communication devices,
heard from the background, ad-speak in transliteration
affirms that we are so much more advanced
than the living deciduous woodlands
who annually bare their well-appendaged trunks
when left unburnt.
My own rootless wandering
turns kerf into dust
and logs into ash
even though
live trees bury their own
input devices for stability
and support. Some provide
offspring even through fire
and all burrow to cappilate
their own sustenance.
The root forms and feeds
the cellulose base
from which all seasonal glory
blooms, flowers and leaves.
The polkas pump a carousel.

Regent's Park

I was happy not to be alone,
but rather with you in Regent's Park.
You waved the web-footed birds
to come ashore for food, heaved handfuls
of broken bread to feed the fowl beside the water.
Together we walked on warm wet pavement,
many months before my heart began
to stop working properly.

Now, you are my winter's expiration,
my long lasting snow,
my release from dissipation,
my expatriation,
as I knuckle under
from the punches of paltry baggage.

The sweet refreshment of my nose
on your neck, my lips curled
on your collarbone, your palms
pushing my shoulders away
as your fingers tighten their grip…
No one has seen your beauty's deep radiance
in ways that I have known you.
You change magnificently as the years pass by us.

Your needs still want care and concern from another.
Your care and concerns for others
still fill and drain the swells of love.
Still, you choose to meet their needs,
happy with the sparks of life you birthed,
and my grateful heart is happy to share this berth.

Edges Closing In

Origami dragons burrow tight.

Snowplow thumps and clears a driveway,
startles the scraggly buzzard
that warms its wings on a neighbor's chimney.

Frigid wind knifes dry snow
from branches, roofs
and whitened stationary objects.

The air, sharp as bee sting all season,
winters here for three months now.

River of sand slides through the crack in time,
seconds necking down a teardrop stem.

The edges are closing in now,
folding talons grip scavenged eyes.

Many stones kringle under foot,
as I trudge this path of happy destiny.

Bloodwaters of the Passaic

for Ron Bremner

Maybe I'd be happy if I could
just find something to fix.
A broken piece of furniture trim,
or a door latch that won't quite stay closed.

Or an old wooden coat hanger
with a zig-zag metal fastener
that juts out of the dry shrunk joint
holding the shoulder pieces to the hook.

Or wait, is that my reflection
in a mirror, that glassed-black sliver
of a shriveled frame that should be
marked "FRAGILE"?

Maybe I can unshroud the contents
of this package to find instructions
to reassemble this frame,
to put some meat back on these bones,
to feel my life has been of some use.
At the end in hope and gratitude,

Who might I see to greet
at the gate of heaven,
were I even blessed to be there.
In the shifting swirl of souls,
billions, trillions, godzillions
of us earthen refuges!

Peter the Saint scans passports,
birth certificates,
get out of jail cards,
standing at the funnel's spout,
at the brea of the corral,
and checks for his break time,
not missing a beat.

Asymptomatic Asymptote

White house with green trim
green deep as a forest dream

White as the basement smelled bleachy
when wringers dripped clothes dry to hang on the line

Inside the detached garage, hooks hung tools
on cool ash gray walls, cinder blocks
painted white on the yard-facing sides,

green trim around the white wooden doors
and metal-framed window

Inside the garage, above the smooth concrete,
a floored loft to storyboard
the young mind's weekend flights

This is how you do it
Keep your tools sharp and clean

Tape your handles for better grips
Say just what you mean

Thicker Water

So, answer me this,
do bees work in the rain?
In a downpour, do buzzing wings
clear their pixelated facets?
Does drenched pollen
coat all with sticky sweetness?
What you cannot answer for me is this,
what will I leave behind?

Unwashed, I worsened down
a waxy fire pole to sleeve
unbound sheaves
of wrought irony riveted
sideways by puerile hardhats.

I bussed through Brick City,
shopped the streets of Silk City,
bought Keds at the U.S. Rubber
employee store in Passaic. Later on,
I ambled through the Big Apple,
tied tomatoes up with stainless steel stakes
that fell off the truck
from the J&L yard in Wayne.

To tend my raging fireplace,
I still wear the welding gloves
that Annie packed at Lawson's
warehouse in Fairfield.
I painted the wheelbarrow red
In Doc William's old town.

Next my blood backs up,
my breaths stop short,
my wet lungs wheeze.
Fat feet, swollen balls, lost my ass.
One large pill can't dowse
my interruptible sleep.

So I punch out,
rush all the way home
and fly south on vacation.
Thicker waters wash me
on the whisperless streets
of Music City. I look northwest
from our Burnham penthouse
as six scaffolded cranes
wave American flags.
The booms winch plumb cables taut,
a proud display of working capital at rest.

The temperature down here
climbs faster than steel.
Siren arias wail each night
in slow pulsing rhythms,
seven, eight, nine per hour.
They spin urban sonic silk,
smooth dark smiles
evil as bandits
on the Natchez Trace
in Colonial times,
bandits who waited for whiskey
or other currencies of wealth
to pass in transit.
Distilling season was then
but twice a year.

Combs of wax, traps, webs
trawled off the Great Falls' spray,
the Indus, the Tigris, the Dnieper.
Pincer claws encircle the river queen,
four-eyed, six-winged,
a huntress of sweet warmth.
Thunder threads the globe.
Lightning's needle
inks charred flax
awash in gossamer shroud,
swiped right out, carbon dated.

Rough Diamond Under the Lights

for Professor Klein

What I like about Jim
is that he answered the phone
when I called him from left field,
and did not pretend to know who I was.

He shook off the signal
from behind home plate.
Then he stretched, kicked, and twisted
to deliver a strike
that would've put the game away,

but I tipped it foul.
Blue dropped a new,
udder-smooth ball
into catcher's upturned mitt.
Unscuffed, it's tossed into play.

That's when Jim's cold eye
wired a busy signal.
He picked up the rosin bag,
spit a bullet into the mound.
He scuffed the ball,
settled it in his glove.

Before I step back
in the batter's box
to work the count,
I knock my spikes clean,
in case he does remember me.

One way or another,
I will keep calling until he does.

Now I'm a washed canvas
stretched with off-white sizing.
Jim's fill-in-the-blanks brush
screwballs color with meaning
as he knuckles a called "Strike three!"
right passed me.

Then, on my way back to the dugout,
I kick clay dust and flop my sorry ass
down on the bench,
just an abstract sourpuss
scraping unrhymable pigments
from my teeth.

The Rest of Us

Unlike some of us,
Saint Joseph,
you listened
to your heart's voice.
What you heard
was not a proclamation,
trumpeted, written on parchment
and nailed to the city gate.
It was a quiet voice,
an angel's breath
that turned you over
from sleep to find her,
full and ripe
with the world's salvation.
That you brought them home
safe from Egypt,
we thank thee.

Declination

My world revolves
around your blooming core,
your profusion of starry heat.
Tethered thus, I dance beneath
your phased reflections,
ducking under your swelling scythe,
bumping against your gibbous bulge.

You have taken my measure,
my direction, my speed.
You have seen my veer
from true north,
and marked my declension from the pole star.

You twirled frost-light
into intergalactic splatter,
you found this emotional,
subjective primate
derailed, off-track, error-spun
with rounded decibels.

My deepest fears gravitate
from within dark lodes,
fears that my worthless dross
will never suffice
to love you Always and Forever,
until, mercy! your lips
spray nova shine in a rising arc.

The phases of your smile
rotate shadows
through my precious,
fragmentary remains,
elliptically aglow
with gratitude and hope.

Why Is Uranus Blue?

Is it molecular hydrogen? Atomic helium?
No, I think not. NASA reports
that traces of atmospheric methane
absorb red wavelengths from solar energy
and bounce blue light back through space,
that vinyl veneer. Please, let's not forget
that there is ammonia too in the hot, dense fluids
that hover over Uranus' small, rocky core.
As gas giants go,
this one is so far from home
that no one drops by to visit.
Sad to say, there's not much else
to support life on the planet either.

Sun Off a Beach

Forget about your gorgeous tan.
The Cloud is much too large to let
sunlight bronze your breast and buttock.

Not only is our earth a-spin
elooping the flames of Helios
but polar tips of frozen oceans

shed shelves of icy calves,
shook warm to drift and float afield.
The sea is rising.

Levitating liquidity dissolves our shores,
scours, devours stubs of scabrous stone,
as pumped sedimentary remnants

are deposed for the sake of your assache parked.
Oh, save us fossil fools, sitting in stuck traffic.
We are stunned, I tell you, simply *stunned* to learn

that we no longer need high-digit SPF's.
No longer will rays of day burn skin & leaf.
Moist brown air holds all the light we need.

Neither can it be created nor be destroyed
but only will its shape shift again, its frame reform,
its land unscape, your tan unline…

Molten Pools

1.
Raise the bar.
Just because we name it elemental
does not make it so.
Unruffled, the feminine sides of my nature
prefer for some things to remain the same:
minted coin stamps, pressed rivets,
pure bullion, unalloyed feed stocks.
Be these in gibbous, crescent, or caloric stasis,
my manly side would make them change
like coins on edge, spinning, balanced on this,
our tilted sphere.
I would raise these high,
unto immobile global transcendence,
a sacrificial host of nodal exchange
held quiet, while seculars educe Eden
from the first few bars of the score unfinished.

Were the spin to stop—either friction
forces the turning coin to fail,
or, pied, the planet coughs to a stop,
spewing subjunctive reflux—
then we'd lose those cool breezes
that prevent the season of rotisserie
from boiling the barrel's bottom.

Tempered thus, crystallinity insurrects without hope.
Atmospheric insensitivity turns water into dust,
dry buoys bear inattentive prognosticators,
yoked to forward-facing logs.

Digits advance the dayspan, drug fast
while light emitting, dies old.
The golden claws sweep faster than before.
The same twelve-hour shift times two rings brass balls
for another new round, but locks it, ratcheted
without return, to the fore morrow,
done before the second bell.

2.
We wants it to last forever, we does.
If we dries the fruit, we keeps it longer
from seed to grape to raisin.
Condensation nation,
the rain's a-coming to ya, humanity.
You were the favorite, Gaia's bloom.
But too sweet to last, you are.
When the swept claws unwind,
the ebbing tide racks vessels sideways,
raising sand, barring none.

Once we was backed by silver or gold,
but our standards dropped, our myths devolved.
A solid dated con plies notes,
unscripted in cuneiform or cursive,
from a stylus dipped in tears.
We gots to trust somebody.
We gots to trust somebody child,
do we got somebody to trust?

3.
World peace contested, every place infested, clichés amiss,
armed forces distracted, filthy masses disinfected.
Welcome to Hideous City, home of the Most Heinous Anus,
whose elemental wholeness and eye weakness news
draw uncrossed vision to interpret the Lost Keys.

Place the SKELETON under the overpass
next to the CHURCH.
Open the GARAGE
without the CODE.
Wander amidst the mangrove swamps.
Wait for, then watch, the sunset.

Move, then remove your collected phone books.
List numeric landlines as they cloud supremely
the world's lost judgment.

Seriously, cloth is not clothes.
Close is not closed.
Tree shadows on Garret Mountain
drip silkworms into paddies east
of eaten at the Hot Grill.

Ingot we trust.

Return Of the Cranes

Winter's tail,
this early March.

December's
sudden pay off

swings new life,
cantilevered

across the horizon.

Compressor hisses
like high-hat cymbals

punching closed!
As an operator's

jackhammer seeds
the asphalt egg:

an embryonic high rise!

Sawyers, Lawyers, Voyeurs

Can you imagine!
If you wanted to back up
an automobile in the last century,
you actually had to turn your head around
to look and see where you were going.
We might as well have called it a pushcart.

Now, it is so much simpler.
We transport vehicles simply
by pushing buttons.
This is automatic mobility.

But while this may appear to be legal
and certainly frees your attention
to handle other contextual challenges,
one potential problem with perpetuating motion
through the use of vehicular awareness prosthetics
is that today's cars
have more mirrors than brains.

So, you might ask,
will the self-driving car
lead to the death of the self?
Then again, you might not.
Stay tuned.
That *would* be a big step,
A real neck stretcher, that one.

And speaking of stretching,
would you like to look back
more than a few centuries?

Then just open a book
and let your mind open.
Who knows what you will see there,
and be amazed. After all,
our first time machine
was arguably the printing press.
Still functional, look what it brought to us:
one way forward, one way back.
Want to go forward?
Turn the page.
Want to go back?
Turn the page.
Want to be transported
to a place not yet made?
Dive into a book, numb nuts,
headfirst!

If you think for a second
that your nanometric transfibulator
will deconstruct the proper dose
of dimethyl poo-poo into fuel
for you to cruise the fourth dimension,
then you are cutting cornices
just to spite your façade.

And be advised!
Around here, you are either
a riser or a tread.
Please remain vigilant,
because this neighborhood
was de-signed
by certified naysayers.
You *will* need to watch out,
if you want to get where you are going.

Lights Action Cam

Before excavating their backyard
to build a deep blue in-ground pool,
new owners of a house up the hill
cut down the big old hemlock hedge
that backdropped their property.

They framed a big deck
across the back of the house too.
Now their view overlooks
other neighbors' yards.
The deck rail is ringed with bulbs,
bright white to footlight
the safe edges of happiness.

Down here below, we love the visual span
when sights unfurl to dry their bathing clan.
The one drawback we cannot close the curtains on
is this. The set is ready noon or night,
lights on forever whether needed or not.

Snapshot

For a dismal several years now,
the parking lot
behind the apartment buildings
has been full of cars.
Workers from home test positive
for normal in their no longer
new-to-remote situations.
Hand-held extraterrestrial devices
drone incessantly on,
as exploration of the universe
slips the world into pocket-sized simulations.

In her quiet hours after school,
a young She-urchin
YouTubed how to develop images
from old celluloid negatives,
even though she failed
her Zoom class in mind reading.

What is a negative, asks the child.
The barest of threads
hold the seat of her pants
together. Hanging tight
by the skin of her teeth
and the strength of her gaze,
she walks to the Grand Union
and buys hot dogs, condiments
and lobster rolls, on sale.
Her cash payment complicates
the self-service check-out.

Outside the emptied grocery store,
a neighborhood Neanderthal
with no-drag knuckles
compliments She-urchin
on her overstuffed peepers.
He sifts irrespirable fibers
off his pleated blue mask,
and bemoans to no one in particular
that the likelihood of cure
will be invaluable.

What is invaluable, asks the child.
Does it mean, unable to be valued,
and therefore, has no value?
She does not know who'd be able
to use it if it had none, nor where.

If the likelihood of cure does have value,
could it mean well for her or her tribe?
Would such a cure keep make-shift morgues
from crossing their ancient burial grounds?
Young She-urchin gets the picture
and bristles at these worn-thin thoughts.
Neanderthal blinks away from her,
more unsure than ever.

She-urchin also learned online
that in Lincoln's time,
reading was thought
to be lazy and indolent.
Now, her phone apps
update automatically
to dismember that
once-popular perception,

which, to the partly illiterate,
remains slightly enlarged
but basically true,
here in this land
where new images
can still develop
chemically
from filtered light.

Harriman Lament

for Michael Shagawat, 1954-1976

Bereft of breath,
the vital spirit that you labored so painfully for,
your prana extinguished, consumed, karma expired.
It's been years since we buried you south of Paterson.
Your mother, sister and brother, your stepfather,
friends and relatives, each sucked into
the maelstrom your departed presence spun
through our all too suddenly too-related lives.
We'd all heard of one another from you,
even if we hadn't met.

You talked about your mother,
how she tried to make it with your father
deceased for many years, how she struggled with
the pain of her own growth, her remarriage.
Your sister's blossoming adolescence fulfilled
ancestral dreams of Middle Eastern beauty.
Your brother could hardly see for all his tears,
supporting your mother on their way to the plot.
I remember you telling me how
he grew into more mature concerns
as the Peace Movement died; how you sighed,
accepting his decisions; your love and respect for him.
Carl, your roommate, was everywhere, doing all he could for
      your family.
Those closest to you all there, skins bared,
exposed by knowing your expired life
to be our loss, your life gone missing,
the life you battled for daily on the street.

New York is no easy town, yet you brought daylight,
gave life to the city's homeless children—
who told your kids you would not be coming back to them,
how? Would they ever know how you watched their sleeping
          heads
hot as glowing coals on long summer nights near the East River?
Did they ever hear your work boots' steady strut to the uptown
          trains
when you made your way home from the shelter in those early,
          early mornings,
your twisting mind finally relaxed with kif-stained melodies,
fluting around the metallic rocking subway roll, Bronx-bound?
Under and over Jerome Avenue, what a line, what a line.
The subterranean subway ride suddenly elevated to glide
through the end of night. Neon stars stretched out, splayed in all
          directions,
a sour Milky Way some dumb giant kicked over as he went out
          to take in the paper,
half asleep and running late in a titan supernatural rat race
where he picks little kids off bean stalks to take and sprout 'em,
gives them lots of water, lots of love, let them grow
on their own, give them some kind of home…

I did see you tiring of your job, though. One cold Fall day
on your scant vacation, you flew in from Denver
and found me in my sleaze-bag rooming house,
on South Willow Street, downtown Montclair.
You were gearing up, ready for a change.
We kicked around taking a trip in the Spring,
but you wouldn't live to see the next Winter.
New Orleans never did see our painted faces on Fat Tuesday.
We never took that travel test which proves or fails friendship,
never took it for more than a long weekend or two,
or a camping trip so far out, man, that
Mahavishnu Birds of Fire had to fly us home!

Another path was yours, my friend.
The fire, the liquid gems
burning behind your eyes,
it took that Catskill Mountain
lake to put them out,
to knock your pipe
empty one last time
and dowse the coals,
to quiet the wind in your sails
and take you from us all.

Close Call

If this were another country,
the radiologist would not have felt
your stubbly armpit as he moved
the lump to see if more pictures were required.

If this were another country,
we might never even have found
the lump, or if we did, might not
have known what it could have meant.

Since this is no other country,
your non-smoking nostrils sigh with
mentholated relief.

The technician observes the doctor's
not-too-concerned-about-it response
to your high-tech exam, with the accent
on not-too-concerned.

If this were another country,
no accent might be noticed.
You might not have quit.

Windy Like Aruba Here on Mother's Day

You rest with my father
across from the beach club.
Traffic on Grove Street rolls by
like breakers down the shore.

Breezes brush my ears,
dabbing voices of other
cemetery visitors
with sand chair chatter.

Thirty-three years since we celebrated
this day with you in person by the sea.
Since then, your stone facing west
winces when I bring you up to date.

We Went to Department Stores Before the Holidays

Sitting in the back of our seatbeltless Ford Falcon station wagon,
all that I wanted to do was look out the hand-cranked window
at the trees and cliffs that Route 46 was cut through and fly up
    the ramp
to throw exactly ten-cents at the toll booth to get on the
    Parkway North
and exit at Route 4 East. We had to go Christmas shopping
at the Garden State Mall in Paramus.

My sister won't stop pulling the back of my crew cut,
so after I knucklepunch her in the arm to make her stop,
my mother tells me through gritted teeth and death eyes
in the rear-view mirror that if I don't knock it off
RIGHT THIS MINUTE,
she'll hit me so hard I won't be able to sit for a week.

Well okay, once in a while I do like to sit down, so I turn back
to looking out at what I can imagine from the sights
of Bergen County. A colorless reel of old reruns fades boredom
    to black.
God, I hate to go shopping. Finally we get there.
Mom parks the car ten miles from the door.
She makes us walk, not run, into Bambergers.

No matter if cold or not outside, my coat is half off
by the time we get in the store, where we charge
into our seasonal ritual of hide and seek
between racks of clothes, around bins and behind counters
full of stuff we can't even fit into, much less care about.

Boy, my head still aches when I remember the blast of
heat that hit you as you walked into the space between the
     doors.
In those days, malls were just big stores disconnected from each
     other
and you had to leave one store to go to the other,
just like down on Market Street. You got headache after
     headache.

This one particular year, my sister ties her coat arms together
in a mammoth wooly knot, slings it like a mace
or a stocking with a lump of coal to crack the top of my skull.
Hah HAH! She chortles, GOT YOU BACK!
Merry Christmas brother! HO HO HO . . .

Wipe Out

For Eddie Infald

The sounds
from Ricky's house
broke loud and tight,
drum skins beaten,
running sticks in flight.
Minutes before,
Ricky's Mom had backed
her blue Corvair
out of their driveway
with her top down,
and raced away fast,
tearing up Carlton Place
like she left her groceries at Shop Rite—
no! worse! —
like she forgot to buy her groceries
last week, and her cupboards were bare!

Shortly after
the blue convertible
peeled out,
Davey Brown
came bopping down
Van Breeman Court
on his way to Ricky's house
around the corner,
with his guitar case
slung over his shoulder.
Minutes later, we heard
the drum set rev up and roll

like the tide turning on us,
drums crushing our neighborhood quiet,
cascading from snare to tom-tom
as cymbals crashed
through the walls of Ricky's house.

The street's silence
was all but shattered
as Davey's fingers
rode waves down the fretboard,
spilling bubbles of salt-slick foam
across wet hard sand,
until the undertow sucked them
licks back under water,
rocks and rolling,
set after set of waves,
building, cresting, curling—hot dogging
on the edge to break pounding
on endless, hidden bars of sand.
Drum sticks gunning solo,
then in tandem
with Fender magic,
amping up
until teenage testosterone
hit Mach 1,
launched through the stratosphere,
and cracked the speed of sound!

Receipt

berserk perverse passions
boil the blood.

trails blaze,
both ends burning.
hands turn up
in desperate yearning.

blood

              smokes,
more   or
          less.

in the flesh of your actions,
there, meat swims,
chucks of touch
stewing the mind.

If End When

If my life was poetry,
my house would dwell
nestled on a rocky outcrop
of bracken-crusted seashore,
on a peninsular thrust
held firm by brushing waves
that slide up and recede
with each pulsing beat
of the ocean's heart.

If my life was poetry,
I'd whittle time to unburnt embers,
wearing little more than skin
that lets me sprout horns or feathers
should the winds chance decide
to blow me down or prod my back
with a suggestive updraft.

If my life were poetry,
my beard would wag
tempestuously
beneath my chin,
a hirsute canyon
from whence my echoes roar.

But no,
my poems keep falling
from the trees of light,
dripped with seabreeze
to dry in salt.

Silver air splashes
across aging footprints
paced in sand,
waits and prays
for gentle rain
to wash and seal
this battered frame.

Short Steps, Long Shadows: The Fourth Law of Thermodynamics

Bad trees get turned into telephone poles.
Instead of storing carbon and freeing oxygen,
naughty cellulose towers are felled, trimmed,
straightened and preserved into an economic useful life.

They are put into service to reliably shoulder
wire and cable, beneficially enslaved to connect
the ultimate energy derivative with devices
that enable convenience and leverage control over expended
      energy.

Generations of higher evolved life forms
eventually found their ways up and onto mapless limbs,
sheltered under leafy canopies and nested in sumptuous hollows.
Old trees drop their deadwood.

Primitive primates miraculously connected found fuel
to fire and soon, temperate woodlands were fielded to feed
Cro-Magnon cranial creations, from flames to frames
to fabricate frivolous affirmations of the fabulous future.

From forks to flat roofs, trees
were transubstantiated from life forms
into eternal beings, unable to oppose their destiny
or offer alternatives to axe or saw.

As industrial evolution extracted riches from the earth
and forces sought ever more efficient multipliers,
so came electric power distribution to thin the herds
of strong straight wood into rate-based fixtures.

And thus did disentropic desires skid the ultimate cooling
of that which changes, and sought to cease what creates or
      destroys,
only to preserve what might be,
beyond the shadow of doubt.

Marbles Lost

1.
Gradually, long ago, glacial plates
curled, then cured
miles of plasmic calcite,
mineral folds from
random metamorphoses,
melded into tectonic permanence.
The planet churned before
tribal grunts ever chorused
around a fire to acknowledge
collective recollections,
well before quarried monuments
ever felt a tradesman's crafty blade.

Yet still it's here.
As I pass their empty house,
I say their names,
just their first names.
I see their young faces bright with games
as they were one-quarter century ago.
I call out their monikers
but cannot recall their last names.
Memory's grip slips like snow
off a warming rock face
as sunny days roll on.

2.
Patches of slow turning heat
drip from pits and privates.
Two blocks over,

a road crew in safely seen
lime green shirts
wipes their sweat,
walks into shade,
breaks for lunch
to eat hot soup
on a steamy day.
A hawk screes, noon.

Neighbors move out,
but the street stays the same
and holds its ground.
My son once said
it's all the same street,
and that truth remains
while every street does.

3.
Three thousand miles away,
a wooden road through Gaelic peat beds
has lasted four thousand years since the Bronze Age,
only to be unearthed by modern day archeologists.

Words bend into blue notes,
twist like slow blown glass,
like seismic waves once sculpted ores,
growl like minerals
chisel-struck
in near-term recall.
Heated words whip-crack
thoughtless soundtracks,
set sonic backdrops
for knuckles down games
in Mohenjo-daro.

Thumb shots persevere,
taw knocks cat's eye out of the ring.
Hands hold the empty bag.

72

Reckless Exaltation

Where was I
that my children did not exist,
did not come into my worries,
that their worries were not of me?

When was it
that I left my parents' home to be free,
unfettered by forbidding threats,
loosed from shackles of permissions withheld

but blind to the ruinous consequences
that trauma would bleed
over my loving family?

Across this moth-eaten isthmus,
broken days deleverage
patterned expectations.

Away in Madagascar,
exhalations of an ordinary sinner eclipse
the marquis' masquerade with mascara.

Sowers proclaim 200 sextillion
to be 200 billion trillion, yes,
one and the same!
Yet ever the number of stars eludes,
confuses every curved and crooked
branch of physics, each bent or broken twig
chilled straight, sleeved in snow, cold and still.

Who am I without you
or maybe the better question is
why am I without you?

Like a bubble in fluid
I float through your life.
You pool
all
there is
or needs to be
and I rise,
a globule tight with air,
rolling through your deep,
my fragile surface spinning
against your diverse densities,
commingling fluids,

across complexions
beyond belief,
until what I concede,
conceives.

Jet Lagged from Covid Again

I would like to grow from
not being a good husband
into becoming an imperfect partner,

one who imparts your wishes
into my commands, who does things
when you want and finishes

your plans. Weak and exhausted,
my love runneth under the weather
this past week.

The hole that I left you in could have been
carefully missed, had I not been
so carelessly ignorant and masked
like you asked me to, after we kissed.

Sorry does not cut it, I know.

Healing Stone

for Sue Mandzik Davis

Curved granite chip, bare bottomed,
yellow topped with golden stars and spots

Healthy green script reads
healing

The curve of the stone
fits perfectly
on the top of my right hand web,
my index finger
nestled around the top left edge,
my thumb clasps
the concave yellow face

With this hard thought in hand,
I cannot press keyboards,
stroke a brush or write a word

With this hard thought in hand,
I grip what must be done
before all else fails

With this hard thought in hand,
no mountain stands before me, insurmountable

With this hard thought in hand,
your love holds me true

Indexication

She was losing it. Her wads worth
of long fellows dripped away,
lecherous poetries that began
with secondary schooling.

Never one for building a core,
she was always
enticed by the exotic
yet drawn to the droll.

Released from hyper nation,
elaborately she bore the will of those ill,
but iterated their aspects as built,
rather than charge ahead wooly

knowing nothing but what she meant.
Her waffled pig pressed
indentured toothless savants
onto marred, unkempt surfaces.

The power went out, now what.
Where's that current?
Your phone is dead. Your internet is gone.

Across a chorus of crossed vocal chords,
a trader's coarse growl barks in open outcry,
"Where's the market?"

Fish whims,
pulled by fins, pushed by gills,
alight on deflected currents.

Eclipses regulate daytime astronomers
captivated by the brightest star
or a tailspun moon.

Beliefs beyond her excessive expectations
detailed deliberated determinations,
as the denouement dissolved
her fundamentalized foundations.
Class dismissed.

No Wrong Way to Eat a Jelly Donut

Doctor tells me that I am lucky
to still be alive, he tells me,
then sends me his bill.

What is the forecast, I ask him
knowingly. Expect, he says,
varying degrees of sunlight
over the next twenty-four hours
with occasional showers
to roll across the sky,
and periods of intermittent darkness.

I could be mistaken,
but I thought I heard this before.

Ideas drop on a puddle,
occasional gasping bubbles
bounce like a diver
pushing up for air.

My first job had me up
at four in the morning
to work as a baker's helper.

One teenaged summer
before I got my license,
my grandmother got my sister and I jobs
at the Saddle Brook Pastry Shoppe
where Grandma was a sales girl up front.

We stayed in her house in East Paterson and she drove us back
        & forth to work
in the blue '69 Buick Skylark
that my grandfather had barely broke in
before he died. Grandma had to take driving lessons to get her
        license.
She knew how to get anywhere from Passaic to Paterson by bus,
but the little widow only drove
the big blue car to the supermarket, church, work and the
        cemetery.
I think it only had seat belts in the front.

Inside the bakery, hot ovens were intense. Frank the foreman
        screamed
at the baker making bread,
"Capo doste Calabrese!"
Jimmy the Greek taught me
to fry and fill donuts
as he laughed at my tired yawns.
"Sleep in car?" He smirked to know
my romantic escapades were still masturbatory secrets,
with hair barely fuzzing my groin.
Old man Retz owned the pastry shoppe
and usually showed up unannounced
to rattle his workers' chains.

I learned to fill donuts
with a two-handed pump
on a five-gallon bucket
of raspberry jelly.

My handiwork was
so sweet and delicious
that I never tired of that taste.

Fifty-five years later
I finally saw the p in raspberry.
Must've been something I ate.

Eggshell Floor

for Matthew Maffey, DO

Visitors tread lightly
where yellow-wristed fall risks
call for help to shuffle.
Scrubbed wizard-fingers
unfold knotted fibers.
White-coated healers
wrap maladies
with molecular magic.
Orderly persons move
stretchers of strain
on wheels of ease
through vertical tunnels,
over polished concrete.
Intensity of care
varies inversely
with somnolent hours.
Here, cures are prep to rest & rehab.

Acknowledgments

Grateful acknowledgment is made to the editors of the following publications, where these poems first appeared:

Journal of New Jersey Poets: "Frozen Funds" (Honorable Mention, 2016 New Jersey Poets Prize)
Painted Poetry: "Time's Mirror"
Rhyme & Punishment NY, NJ, CT: "Why Is Uranus Blue?"
The Rutherford Red Wheelbarrow: "Back to Normal," "Backspace," "Black Friday," "Chance of Passing," "Edges Closing In," "From a Lockward Prompt," "Healing Stone," "Knowing Where the Dream Ends," "Lunch with Jimmy Sturr," "Marbles Lost," "Oval Sex," "Regent's Park" (2022 Pushcart Prize Nominee), "The Lost Word," "Thicker Water," "To Marion of Lion's Teeth," "Turkey Buzzard Tower," and "Wax Waned"
The Stillwater Review: "More Shirts Than Money," "If End When"
Voices From Here 2: "On 'Oh'"
Vox Poetica: "Highland Fling"

www.ingramcontent.com/pod-product-compliance
Lightning Source LLC
Chambersburg PA
CBHW061438160726
47995CB00003B/939